Tiger Woods

Ten Ways
to
Play the Lie

To Carol
Hope this
makes you laugh

2010

Citizen Poet Takes on . . .

Tiger Woods

Ten Ways
to
Play the Lie

Dan Speers

Author Contact: danspeers@CitizenPoet.com
Official website: www.CitizenPoet.com

Electronic Editions: Essential10 Ltd.
15400 W 64th Avenue
9E-147
Arvada, CO 80007-6852

eCopies – All Versions
www.Essential10.com

Kindle Edition
ASIN: B0032AM9U4

Print Edition: CreateSpace
ISBN: 1450545580
EAN-13: 9781450545587

www.CreateSpace.com

Hockey is a sport for white men. Basketball is a sport for black men. Golf is a sport for white men dressed like black pimps.

—Tiger Woods

Citizen Poet Takes on

Tiger Woods:
Ten Ways to Play the Lie

Table of Contents

Introduction

Tiger Woods says to make your goal
A pro must strive to "feel" each hole.

Golf Quip: Winston Churchill once said that he could "never believe in a game where the one who hits the ball least wins."

In a year in which famous men like John Edwards, Mark Sanford, David Letterman and a number of other wealthy, famous and powerful men admitted cheating on their wives, it still came as a shock when the numerous affairs of Tiger Woods suddenly came to light.

Surely, not Tiger, was the visceral reaction. Not this fine, upstanding symbol of clean-cut sportsmanship and athletic prowess. It was hard to imagine—especially since one of his female companions alleged that Woods had also engaged in a bisexual relationship.

Woods not only made his name in golf, he helped make golf a popular and exciting game. Of course, golf itself is a game of contradictions. Although it started as a rich man's sport, there is little question, as the old saw goes, that it is now a game with millions of poor players. And many of them are fans of Tiger Woods. If not lovers.

As the story unfolds, Citizen Poet examines both the man and the game, investigating both the similarities and contrasts between golf and sex. And, of course, we have taken our usual liberties with poetic license.

1. A Bad Lie

On Tigers Woods we can rely,
Even Pros can have a bad lie.

Golf Quip: "Isn't it fun to go out on a course and lie in the sun?" – Bob Hope.

Ten Reasons Tigers Become Cheetahs:
No. 1. The Rush of Risk; Thrill of the Chase

For athletes of the caliber and fame of Tiger Woods, infidelity can be a high stakes game and there is some evidence that it provides the same high-octane adrenaline rush that comes from competitive, high-risk sports.

It takes subterfuge, the finagling and juggling of schedules and locations, and often intricate conspiracies with trusted friends to keep the affairs secret from both the wife and the public, as well as multiple mistresses or lovers, both paid and otherwise.

The greater the number of lovers, particularly female lovers, the greater the indication that the thrill of the chase may be even more satisfying than the actual consummation, although consummation is certainly one way of keeping score.

Name Your Tool: God's club

The 1-iron. It's called God's club because God only knows how to use this club correctly.

Jim Murray, Pulitzer Prize-winning columnist for the Los Angeles Times, has written that the only time he took out a 1-iron was to kill a tarantula.

Even so, the 1-iron has had it moments, especially for one of the most famous photographs in golf history, that of Ben Hogan using the club to hit into the 18th green at Merion to the win the 1950 U.S. Open.

The Tiger Woods Golf Dictionary

Afraid of the Dark. 1. A putt that refuses to go into a hole. 2. An excuse used by a mistress for keeping the lights on during a tryst, despite the ease of taking surreptitious cell phone pictures.

Age Players. 1. Playing 18 holes with a score equal to one's age. 2. Acting one's age while playing 18 holes.

Back Door. A hole entered from the rear, usually after it appeared there was no chance to enter from the front. This often occurs after a putt curves around a hole and slips in the back way, much like a husband sneaking back home in the wee hours of the morning.

> **Back Doors, Famous.** The putt by Spain's Steve Ballesteros that defeated Tom Watson on the seventy-second hole of the 1984 British Open Championship at St. Andrews.

Back Nine. Final 27 holes of an 18-hole golf course.

2. Something's a Miss

For Tiger Woods, a mistress
Is what seems to be a Miss
Between him and his mattress.

Golf Quip: "Golf is like love," according to Robert Di Vincenzo. "One day you think you're too old. The next day you want to do it again."

Ten Reasons Tigers Become Cheetahs:
No. 2. *Endless Opportunities to Play Around*

Many golfing professionals are the rock stars of their world. Like popular musicians, famous actors, comics, writers and media personalities, they are feted, pampered and adored by legions of fans. And there are plenty of fans who want to share a part of that fame, both emotional and physical.

Golf has grown from a popular sport to entertainment with reporters comparing Annika Sorenstam to Alice Cooper and Tiger Woods to Mick Jagger.

To many, there is little difference between pop culture, celebrities, and brands. Sports figures like Tom Brady, Kobe Bryant, Tiger Woods, Payton Manning and Serena Williams are as famous and sought after as George Clooney, Jon Bon Jovi, Brittany Spears or Paris Hilton.

Given the intoxication of fame and fortune for both star and fan, from casual meetings in bars to parties and even "arranged" liaisons, there is no shortage of willing partners for anything from a few minutes of intimate contact to extended relations.

Name Your Tool: The brassie

The 2-wood. At one time, the sole of the 2-wood was made of brass as are, according to the rumor mills, Tiger Woods' balls.

The Tiger Woods Golf Dictionary

Backside (syn. Backdoor). 1. The side of the cup opposite the position of a player's ball on the green. 2. A term referring to a portion of the anatomy sometimes involved in straight sex and nearly always in gay encounters.

Bail out. 1. Hitting a ball in a particular direction in order to avoid a hazard. 2. Exiting a golf cart if, after calling into work sick, one later spots the boss on the course.

Backswing. That portion of the swing occurring after the ball has been improperly addressed but prior to the ball's disappearing into the rough.

Ballwasher. 1. A noise-making device designed to unnerve an opponent. 2. Any commode located in golf course restrooms.

Barky. Making par when the shot involves a tree and a junk bet.

3. Playing a Round

They say Tiger Woods played a round,
Another nineteenth hole he found.

Golf Quip: NHL goalie Gerry Chevers once said that his golf game was ". . . one under. One under a tree, one under a rock, one under a bush . . .."

Ten Reasons Tigers Become Cheetahs:
No. 3. Because They Can, a Sense of Entitlement

Many rich and famous men from sports to business to politics to creative arts cheat on their wives simply because they can, or rather, they have the opportunities and the means to cheat without encumbrances.

The fewer responsibilities or obligations, the fewer restraints there are to one's extracurricular activities. When one doesn't need a reason to cheat, it is hard to imagine a reason why one shouldn't cheat.

Wealth and fame are not only powerful aphrodisiacs but intoxicating as well. Many of these powerful men feel that they can cheat and get away with it because of who they are and how other people relate to them.

Every politician knows the danger of sexual dalliance, yet there is no shortage of powerful and influential politicians who have who have been caught up in scandal. And just as politicians can go astray, so can sports heroes.

One thing all of these men have in common is that they regard themselves as being exempt from the rules and moral constraints that apply to the rest of us. At the very least, these men all seem to regard infidelity as no big deal.

Name Your Tool: The spoon

The 3-wood. Formerly a wooden-shafted club with concave club face. Modern clubs are no longer spoon-faced but do have a small head and a long shaft. You will most often find a 3-wood snugly tucked into the rear of a golf bag.

Note: It is a well-known, scientific fact that all 3-woods are possessed by demons.

The Tiger Woods Golf Dictionary

Be the ball. A phrase used by actor Chevy Chase in the classic golfing movie, *Caddyshack,* and adopted by neophytes who imagine they can become golf pros by "feeling" the game or in some cases, "feeling" the balls.

Beach. 1. Sand-filled bunkers and other sand-covered areas on a golf course. 2. A caddy's ex-wife or girlfriend.

Bent. 1. A golf club formerly employed in attempting to make a particularly difficult shot that failed. 2. The type of grass planted on greens. 3. A player who either prefers to play with members of his own sex or who has the ability to swing both ways.

Birdie. 1. A score on a hole that is one stroke below par. 2. 20-foot "gimme" putt. 3. The best of one or more practice swings. 4. A Mulligan. 5. The little snitch that tells a player's spouse about their mate's affair.

Blind Hole. A green and hole that are out of sight on the approach, requiring the golfer to rely on his sense of the course, his knowledge of golf, and after hitting the ball, the occasional scream of an unseen player in an earlier group.

Bob Barker. A shot hit high enough to earn the immortal works snickered by one of your partners, "Come on down."

Bogey. **1.** A score of one over par on any hole. **2.** The number of strokes required to finish a hole in a friendly game. 3. **Double-bogey.** Two strokes over par. 4. **Bogey train.** A series of consecutive bogeys, usually the result of excessive dependence on refreshments (*see* **Cart girl**).

Bunker. 1. Holes dug in golf courses, filled with sand or quicklime and intended to attract golf balls and trap golfers. 2. Extremely large bunkers are referred to as condominiums. 3. A hazard in Florida where a number of golfers have been permanently interred or at least kept long enough to start receiving letters with WWII APO addresses.

Bomb. 1. A long drive by Tiger Woods. 2. A strong marijuana cigaret. 3. **Bombed**. Under the influence.

Break. 1. The point where the direction of a putt changes due to the slant or a dip in a green. 2. A spot on Tiger Woods head and/or in the windshield of his car brought about by his wife wielding a club after reading a secret cell phone message from one of his mistresses.

Caddy. The person who carries a player's golf bag and offers advice on what club to use in a particular situation and whether it is during or after a match.

Can. 1. The hole. The cup. The hole in the ground where one puts putts but only a putz puts putz. 2. A privy.

Cart girl. The young lady who drives the beer cart around the course offering very expensive beverages to very thirsty golfers. Despite fantasies, the cart girl has never been known to putt out on a green.

Central American putt. 1. A putt that requires one more revolution in order to fall into the cup. 2. A place other than the Appalachian Trail where Gov. Mark Sanford of South Carolina plays with his balls.

Chili dip. 1. Hitting the ground during a chip shot just before contact with the ball, sending shock waves up the shaft and the ball itself only a few inches. 2. An after sex dip in the motel pool with a mistress.

Chip Shot. A short, low approach shot that positions the ball for one or more bogeys.

Comebacker. 1. A shot that backs up after hitting the green. 2. A tee shot that hits one of the tee markers and ends up behind you. 3. What the PGA desperately hoped for during the period Tiger Woods was missing after the initial news of his affairs.

Competition. 1. The rules, form of play, methods, and conduct established to govern the act of competing for profit or a prize. 2. An event in which a winner is selected from among two or more contestants. 3. The contestant one hopes to defeat. 4. An event in which the winner is the player having better lies than the other contestants.

Cup. 1. Technically, it's the plastic or metal cylinder fitted into the hole, but players typically just say "cup." 2. One way of identifying waitresses, beer cart girls, and mistresses, as in D, Double-D, or kawangas.

4. Hits and Misses

Tiger Woods, famed for hits and misses,
We know the hits came from his Mrs.,
But the count on misses still amasses.

Golf Quip: "Golf is a game where the ball lies poorly, and the players well." - Anonymous.

Ten Reasons Tigers Become Cheetahs:
No. 4. *Peer Pressure and a Little Help*
from One's Friends

Very few men would admit that they cheat on their wives because their friends or teammates expect or encourage them to, but then, there is no question that some men would not feel comfortable letting their friends find out that they failed an opportunity to bed a beautiful, willing woman.

In some circles, promiscuity implies masculinity and if a man moves in circles where his friends are cheating or are promiscuous, then the power of peer pressure is such that he likely will soon be cheating as well. If he cheats and shares his experience with his friends, then he will probably do it again. And again.

Many affairs are facilitated by friends who offer homes and apartments for trysts, set up meetings and lie to the wives of their friends to provide cover.

Tiger's bodyguards were said to have arranged women for him. Tiger's childhood friend was alleged to have arranged the airfare and hotel for Rachel Uchitel to meet Tiger in Australia.

Name Your Tool: The baffle

The 4-wood. Formerly a 5-wood. 1. A golf club head that includes a hollow body and a side hole. 2. Any of a series of occasional baffles or mountings possessing a high memory retention and openings that can be adjusted to fit all standard shaft diameters.

The Tiger Woods Golf Dictionary

Die (or, **dying) in the hole.** 1. Putting a ball so that it falls into the cup just as it is losing its momentum, or *dying*. 2. A situation calling for Viagra.

Divot. A catch-all Scottish term for a different sized pieces of turf scooped from the ground during an iron shot. The actual terms include the:
- *wee tuffie*, 2"x4";
- *peg o' sward*, 4"x6";
- *snatch of haugh*, 6"x8";
- *tussock*, 8"x10";
- *glen*, 1'x2';
- *loch*, suitable for hiding a small monster, and
- *English divot*, approximately the size of an inlet on the Thames.

Dog track. 1. Derogatory term for a golf course that is poorly maintained. 2. An open tournament popular in Florida with older resident golfers and mature groupies.

Dub. A poor shot that rolls on the ground and stops far short of its target. **Dubber**. A duffer who is known for consistently hitting dubs. **Rub-a-Dub.** What a hooker does with a duffer who comes up short in the shaft department.

5. Groupies

Tiger Woods has played in foursomes,
Five-, six- and wow, a lot moresomes.

Golf Quip: According to Dave Hill, the golf swing is like sex. "You can't be thinking about the mechanics of the act while you are performing."

Ten Reasons Tigers Become Cheetahs:
No. 5. Feeling "Special," or Ego Enhancement

Every man likes to feel special, and having uninhibited sex with a beautiful woman can further feed the already overinflated ego of a rich and powerful man.

This is especially true when their new-found partners are willing to engage a variety of sexual activities that would be awkward or difficult with their spouses. In fact, several "other" women report that they deliberately make themselves more exciting and appealing by performing activities that they suspect their partner's wives would shy away from.

Then there is the excitement of successfully arranging the seduction, the reward of being in bed with a new partner willing to engage and explore new worlds of sensuality. Although it could be delusional, an affair can make even rich and famous men feel sought-after and even more powerful.

Name Your Tool: The mashie

The 5-iron. 1. Introduced about 1880 and used for pitching and backspin. Compression and backspin create loft. 2. At the 19th hole, the object of a masher.

The Tiger Woods Golf Dictionary

Eagle. A score two under par for a hole. Like a hole-in-one, most often achieved when playing alone.

Egg. 1. A term for the ball during a putt. One can never hit or chip an egg, but one can roll it. 2. An alibi buddy. 3. What Tiger Woods had on his face after the string of mistresses began to unravel.

Elephant's ass. Any shot that's high and stinky, especially a shot that's higher than it is long. When executed by one's boss, it calls for feigned praise: "Wow. Great direction. A little lower and that would have been a fantastic shot."

Elephants' Burial Ground. 1. Fairways with abrupt hills. 2. Greens studded with mounds where scores go to die.

Etiquette. Courtesy exercised on the course by following the rules against picking up a rolling golf ball, kicking a ball in or out of bounds, announcing the discovery of your ball by surreptitiously dropping another, conceding a chip shot, or posing for a group photo with tees in your nose.

Explosion. 1. A shot that explodes off a wedge and pops out of a sand trap. 2. Otherwise calm and rational players who inexplicably fly off the handle after their ball lands in the rough, out of bounds, in a bunker or water hazard, in a gopher hole, in back of a tree, or the front seat of a Lincoln Continental parked in reserved slot next to the clubhouse.

6. Baring the Wood

Jamie's pix prove Tiger Woods would,
What they show is Tiger Woods' wood.

Golf Quip: "I'm hitting the woods just great, but I'm having a terrible time getting out of them." - Harry Tofcano.

Ten Reasons Tigers Become Cheetahs:
No. 6. Feeling Superior

Very few men rich and famous men would risk their prestige and positions if they knew they were going to get caught, but of course, considering exposure of their dalliances as even a remote possibility represents a contradiction in terms, at least to them. For example, Tiger Woods never suspected that one of his mistresses, Jamie Junger, would tell the world she took pictures of him passed out naked on her sofa.

The fact is, wealth and esteem create an illusion of invincibility, a heightened sense of superiority that proves they can outsmart their wives, the public, the media, their church, their mothers, their children and anyone else they choose to fool, including multiple mistresses.

In many cases, this smugness quickly turns to contrition if and when the miscreants are exposed, but even this self-serving portrayal of regret and penitence is hard for many to accept as genuine.

13

The alternative is to do what Tiger did, which was to withhold any public response. Despite overwhelming curiosity as to the next phase, his public would have to wait to see the ultimate conclusion and when and where he would return to golf.

Name Your Tool: The smashie

Any club wrapped around a tree. Any club flung into a water hazard is a "splashie." One tossed at a dog is a "lassie." A club with a slippery handle or that is used in a somewhat violent manner to express the rage of an irate player is known as a "bashie." A club used to knock out the rear window of a car is known as a "mashie."

The Tiger Woods Golf Dictionary:

Fan. 1. To miss a ball entirely. 2. What a miss does to the balls.

Fighting. Dealing with a golfing flaw as in "fighting a slice, fighting a balky putter, fighting a hook," or "fighting the wife over a hooker."

Finesse. Using an extraordinary means to get out of difficulty, as in using an iron to blast out of sand, a wedge to advance a ball against the wind in a hurricane, or an $80 million offset to a prenuptial agreement to forestall a divorce.

Flagstick. A long pole with a numbered flag at the top that when not left lying on the green by a previous group shows the location of the hole.

Flier lie. 1. A good lie in the rough. 2. First guess on the number of strokes taken on any hole. 3. An excuse tried out with a buddy before using it with one's wife.

14

Fluffy. 1. A ball that is sitting up in or resting on top of the grass, and with some space open underneath the ball. 2. A dog owned by a trophy wife that must fed, sprayed, petted, or walked prior to any intimate activities.

Follow-through. The continuation of the swing after the ball has been hit and prior to the club's being launched into a trajectory on its own.

Fore. 1. One of two four-letter words starting with "F" that are exchanged as an approaching group of players hits balls toward the group preceding them. 2. Foreplay.

Foursome. 1. A group of four playing a round of golf together. 2. A match in which two pairs of players play against each other with each side playing one ball.

> *Fearsome*. Four men playing around of golf together after waiting for their tee time at the 19th hole.

> *Gruesome*. Four exceptionally poor players in one group that is often playing in front of your group.

> *Quarrelsome*. Any group of married couples.

> *Threesome*. Any group of three, male and or female, who play together both on and off the golf course.

> **Twosome**. 1. A pair of players on a golf course. 2. A pair of swingers on a tournament tour.

Fried egg. 1. A ball impacted in a sand trap with the top poking out of a round of sand. 2. A golfer who drinks excessively during a round.

Frosty. 1. A score of 8 on a hole, taken from the nickname of the most famous snowman of them all. 2. Tiger Woods' wife after seeing the caller IDs on his cell phone.

Fuzzy. 1. Greens that need mowing. 2. PGA Tour golfer Frank Urban Zoeller's nickname. 3. *Fuzzies*, pl. What Tiger was bumping with the owners of the names on his caller ID.

Gallery. Tournament spectators who follow their favorite players from hole to hole, often wearing the same outfits, drinking the same drinks, and sometimes known to give their heroes small assists.

Gas. 1. What an egg runs out if it comes up short on a putt. 2. What Tiger Woods ran out of after a short drive into a tree.

Game. 1. A round of golf involving completion. 2. A style of play. 3. A standard based on previous successes or lack thereof, as in, He's on or off of his game.

Goat farm. 1. A poorly maintained course. 2. An exclusive spa or retreat for sexually addicted men. 3. A VFW club.

Gobble. 1. An obsolete slang term meaning a hard-hit putt that holes out. 2. One way to grip a shaft.

Golf accessories. Gadgets that thin a golfer's wallet.

Golf club. 1. A tool consisting of a shaft, head, face and heel and used for hitting balls. 2. A place where one finds a gathering of golf players who also have balls, shafts, heads, faces and heels, although in different locations than are found on the golfing tool.

Grand Slam. 1. The four major championships: The Bristish Open, the U.S. Open, PGA Championship, and the Masters. 2. A hooker and a $1,000 coit.

Grinder. 1. A golfer who is all business and whose objective is achieving the best score. 2. A swinger's dream.

Grip it and rip it. 1. A phrase made popular by John Daly explaining how he won the 1991 PGA title at Crooked Stick with powerful drives. "I just grip it and rip it," he said. 2. To put aside the typical golfing "swing thoughts" and take a healthy rip at the ball. 3. A term for some experienced swingers who play around.

Grow teeth. 1. Plaintive prayer for a ball to step up and grow teeth. 2. Something Tiger Woods was said to have done after he broke fifty for nine holes.

7. Par for the Course

Hi jinx on the links may be fine,
But what's rare is par sixty-nine.

Golf Quip:

Duffer A: What the difference between the sweet-spot and the G-spot?
Duffer B: A man will actually try to find the sweet-spot.

Ten Reasons Tigers Become Cheetahs:
No. 7. Variety As the Spice of Life

Given the lifestyle on the tournament and exhibition circuit, the prevalence of opportunistic sex, especially the opportunity to have sex without getting caught, would certainly explain a lot, but there is a question of consistency involved, especially in the case of Tiger Woods.

There doesn't appear to be a lot of variety in the choice of mistresses and more than one commentator has remarked on Tiger's apparent proclivity for certain attributes. However, the list of alleged mistresses does not appear to represent an effort on his part to satisfy a sexual curiosity about having sex with either a particular person or a random person.

This may leave two reasons why Tiger might try to spice up his sex life. One is to affirm his own sexuality through alliances with women who present an aspect of an imaginary woman that his wife does not. In this case, the variety that he is seeking is not with different women, but in different types of sex or particular sex acts. The second reason might be simply that he needs or desires sex more often than his wife.

Name Your Tool: A jigger

The 4-iron. 1. A club used for chipping and short approaches. 2. What you are expected to buy for everyone at the 19th hole after scoring a hole-in-one, especially if your group is the last to complete a round for the day.

The Tiger Woods Golf Dictionary

Hacker. A golfer who is incredibly bad.

Hand mashie. The five-fingered club attached to the end of a golfer's arm.

Hanging. 1. A lie where the ball is above the golfer's feet. 2. What a golf widow plans for a husband caught in a lie about where his balls were hanging.

Hazard. 1. A man-made obstacle on a course. 2. An overly suspicious spouse.

Head. 1. The end of the club that causes fans, whiffs, hooks, splices, shanks, bollixes and mis-hits. 2. The end of the club that causes blisters, calluses, and wrist sprains. 3. What some golfers expect when playing around.

Home hole. 1. The 18th hole, so called because it the final hole before getting home to the 19th hole. 2. [Incredibly sexist definition deleted by author's wife.]

Hump. 1. The job of a caddy, i.e. to "hump" a pro,s golf bag around the course. 2. What Tiger Woods is said to have done off the course.

8. Hazards on the Back Nine

Girls, bunkers and beer—it all fits.
It explains the sand in their Slitz.

Golf Quip: When asked how in the world he had managed to four-jack (take four putts) a hole at the Masters, Pro Steve Ballesteros answered, "I miss. I miss. I miss. I make."

Ten Reasons Tigers Become Cheetahs:
No. 8. That Old Feeling: Sexual Excitement

One common, invariably self-serving justification for cheating that men cite is a feeling of neglect or being taken for granted, especially after the arrival of children and the family unit involves more than just the honeymoon couple.

Inevitably, the children and the family unit alter the focus of attention and activity, and for athletes with powerful and irrepressible egos, adjusting to this change can be extraordinarily difficult. Spousal sex may become hurried and limited both in location and frequency, which, in turn may lead to performance issues. As noted, Tiger Woods may have sought sex more often.

For the athlete, an affair is a way to restore that old feeling of sexual excitement, regain his preeminence as the center of attention, and restore confidence. As to whether this renewed sense of self-possession and confidence had become evident in Tiger Woods' tours and professional athletic performances, golfing commentators have presented mixed reviews.

Name Your Tool: The niblick

A 9-iron. 1. A name loosely applied to any club with a lofted face such as the 7 to 9, and any wedge despite a greater slope. 2. A term golfers suspect has certain sexual connotations but no one knows exactly what they are. 3. "Niblick, hell. What a man needs in this mosquito hole is Flit." Dr. Seuss and Flit. New Yorker Magazine, August 3, 1929.

The Tiger Woods Golf Dictionary

Iffy lie. 1. Uncertainty about where a ball will travel when whacked by a particular club. 2. Golf scores written in pencil. 3. Tiger Wood's explanation to his wife on what he was doing while on a tournament.

Irons. 1. Metal implements used to torture golfers. 2. Metal implements used to torture prisoners.

Jerk. 1. To pull a shot or putt left of the intended line. 2. Tiger Woods.

Jump. 1. What a ball sometimes does from a flier lie. 2. What Tiger Woods did regarding the bones of a mistress.

Kill. 1. To hit a ball with great force. 2. What Tiger Woods may have done to his marriage.

Legs. A ball that continues to travel a considerable distances after landing. If the ball rolls into water, it has **fins**. If it rings the cup on a putt, it has **lips**. If last seen flying into the tree tops, it has **wings**. Balls shared with a mistress have **alimony**.

Lay. 1. How a ball "lies." 2. What Tiger Woods was said to be looking for before, during and after play.

Lie. 1. The ball described in **Lay**, above. 2. The number of strokes the player says it took to get the ball to where the ball described above now lies.

9. The "Feel" of the Game

"Feel" is Tiger's secret to golf
You might skip taking your clothes off.

Golf Quip: "Although golf was originally restricted to wealthy, overweight Protestants, today it's open to anybody who wears hideous clothing." - Dave Barry.

Golfing pro Jack Issacs, who won the Virginia Open at 42 and qualified for the British Open when over 50, once said "feel" is the total answer in golf. He is said to have recommended interminable practice involving a mattress, a fiber door mat and a living room rug, a combination that is suggested in a variety of situations.

Ten Reasons Tigers Become Cheetahs:
No. 9. Buying into a Woman's Bed, or Out of It

While wealth is a powerful aphrodisiac, it is also a fantastic facilitator. It's no secret that wealthy men use their wealth to attract women and buy their way into a variety of different beds and situations. These men see no reason to buy whomever and whatever they want.

They also often see nothing wrong with discarding whatever they bought as well. And in the unlikely event they are caught or get into trouble, then they can use their wealth to buy their way out of difficulty. The line-up of alleged former mistresses of Tiger Woods seems inordinately punctuated with lawyers and hints of potential remunerations for wrongs imagined or otherwise.

Name Your Tool: Putter

A short-shafted club with a straight face designed for use on a green to produce a shot that rolls a few feet and then stops short of the cup.

The Tiger Woods Golf Dictionary

Lie. 1. Where the ball comes to rest. 2. The number of stokes the player claims that got that particular lie.

Lip. 1. The rim around a cup. 2. Perimeter of grass that surrounds a hole. 3. What you get from your partners if your balls stop there.

Loose impediments. Naturally occurring but non-indigenous objects that are legally movable in order not to interfere with play, such as discarded coffee containers, stunned birds, dazed spectators, disoriented mammals, recent clippings, tree limbs resulting from lightning strikes, and in the case of Tiger Woods, boulders deposited by glaciers during a recent ice age that require entire work crews to move.

Lurking. 1. A competitor in a tournament who seems likely to make a move toward the top of the leader board. 2. The action of a denizen of the 19th hole who has his or her eye on another patron, usually of the opposite sex.

Mark. 1. A small object such as a shotgun shell, coin or tee used to mark the spot where a ball is lifted off the putting green. 2. A poor player who thinks he's pretty good.

Model swing. 1. A totally professional swing. 2. A professional swinger.

Muff. 1. To miss a particular shot. 2. A particular spot on a miss.

Mulligan. 1. A second, provisional ball played from a tee to compensate for low flying planes, excessive gravitational pull of the moon, too much cheer in a previous round, or to replace a lost or unplayable ball. 2. Taking one's mistress along on the honeymoon. 3. A second shot when the first shot has been "muffed."

Nasty. 1. A junk bet that you can hole a shot off the putting green for par or better. 2. What Tiger Woods and his mistresses and other lovers were doing.

Needle. Good-natured ribbing or hectoring designed to get under the skin of an opponent and force him or her to beg either for a Mulligan or a divorce, both of which call for a one-stroke penalty.

Numbers. Scoring. The Net Score is the final score after subtracting the handicap from the Gross Score and is usually only a half dozen or so strokes lower than the actual number of shots made by the player.

OB. 1. A ball that travels out of bounds after struck either by a club or the side of a shoe. 2. An "Oscar Brown" is an OB called by an opposing player with an evil grin and a scruffy shoe. 3. Infidelity.

On Fire! 1. Tiger Woods on a good day in tournament play. 2. Tiger Woods on a bad day in tournament play.

Out of bounds. A ball that while it may appear to be out of bounds, is actually a good 24,900 miles inside the opposite out-of-bounds line when taking both the circumference and curvature of the earth into consideration.

Over cooked that one! 1. A ball too far (i.e. hit the ball over the green.) 2. Tale told by Tiger Woods and his mistress to his wife about their non-affair affair.

Pair. 1. Two golfers playing together in a stroke competition. 2. To assign two players to play together in a competition. 3. What some said Tiger Woods had in order to cheat on his wife. 4. What all of Tiger Woods lovers had, although not necessarily in same body location.

Peg. 1. A tee. 2. A woman not named as a Tiger Woods mistress.

Penalty. One or more strokes added to a golfer's score for a) violating the rules, b) bending the rules, or c) interfering with an opponent's balls.

Play 'em down. 1. To play the ball as it lies. 2. Dismiss rumors about affairs as lies from jealous competitors.

Preferred lie. 1. An implication that a player may have moved his ball to improve his lie. 2. The lie that convinces one's wife that there is no mistress.

Pro Shop. The major hazard on most courses.

Quick. Rushing your swing, putting strokes or overall game. Not to be confused with a **Quickie**, which does not require a tee time, or a **Short Game**, which also involves waffles, waggles, chips, pops, poops, pitches, putts, and sand trap blasts.

Quitting on the ball. 1. Not following through on a shot. 2. Getting a phone call from your wife wondering where you are.

Release. 1, The point in your downswing when you uncock your wrists. 2. The point in swinging when you uncock.

Reload. 1. To tee up a second ball after muffing the first try. 2. A term used to announce the arrival of the beer cart, as in, "Let's reload." 3. To take a short break from swinging practice. 4, To take a short break from swinging.

Road hole. 1. The 17th hole at St. Andrews, said to be the most difficult hole in the world. 2. A hole played while the golfer is out of town or on a tournament.

10. Getting Rid of the Shanks

From hookers, Tiger Woods
should have steered clear,
And left all those shanks attached to a steer.

Golf Quip: Lee Trevino claims the safest way to survive being caught in lightening storm on a golf course is for golfers to hold their 1 iron over their heads because "even God can't hit a one iron."

Ten Reasons Tigers Become Cheetahs:
No. 10. Just Can't Say "No"
or Is It an Addiction?

It is a fair question for a man to ask himself: Could I remain faithful to my wife should I come into fame and fortune and suddenly have unlimited opportunities for sexual high jinx? However, it is probably not fair to expect an honest answer, or at least, an answer that admits to the possibility of temptation.

Let's face it, when surrounded by exotic and intoxicating women offering almost any pleasure imaginable, remaining faithful might require an extraordinary act of will.

Many men, especially those who already feel somewhat elite, are unwilling to dismiss opportunities, especially when their friends or fans are aware of the offer. This is, of course, direct peer pressure, but there may be a deeper cause.

There are some men who are simply unable to say, "No." A number of men find themselves compelled to seek out and consummate at every opportunity—a medical condition defined as sex addiction.

Psychologists appeared on television shows immediately after the Tiger Woods disclosure commenting on the possibility of sexual addiction, citing not only the large number of alleged dalliances, but also the Barbie doll-like similarities between his alliances as indicative of compulsive, questing behaviors.

Pop psychologies aside, many serial cheaters often resort to a claim of sexual addiction, especially after getting caught, and turn to one some form of treatment or rehabilitation to ameliorate their circumstances. In some cases, as has been suggested in that of Tiger Woods, the man may resort to a stay in a sexual addiction treatment center as either a condition of saving his marriage or convincing a judge not to assess an unreasonable marriage settlement.

Name Your Tool: The fibstick, a.k.a. the fablespoon

A "fibstick" is any club that the player used to score a hole-in-one. If the club is a wood, it also may be known as a "fablespoon." Particularly apropos if the player hitting the hole-in-one was playing alone.

Did you hear how God punished a priest who skipped saying Mass one Sunday morning in order to sneak out to the links to play a round of golf by himself? God let the priest hit a hole in one. The priest was ecstatic until he realized his punishment. He could never tell anyone.

The Tiger Woods Golf Dictionary

Rough. 1. Grassy, brushy areas located next to tee off areas, fairways, greens, pipelines, or other nearby hazards. 2. A term that describes how Tiger Woods life is expected to be after reconciliation and his treatment in one or more sexual addiction treatment centers.

Round Robin. 1. Where every player has the opportunity to play with every other player. 2. In golf, it is also a form of tournament play.

Rub of the Green. 1. Interruption of play by causes unrelated to the players or caddies. 2. Bad luck. 3. The sudden appearance of a process server. 4. The use of actual money in the conduct of one's affairs.

Run. 1. When a ball travels on the ground. 2. A player on a roll, good or bad. 3. A player who disappears between the last round and the 19th hole at the clubhouse, usually after losing a particularly large bet. 4. Tiger Woods after holing one too many off of the course.

Sand trap. A bunker or hole in the ground filled with sand and players mired in their own deep depression.

Score. The total number of strokes a player claims for each hole that are then added to produce a gross score from which the handicap is deducted and then reduced by the amount of the tip given the caddy.

Set 'em up. 1. Improving your lie on the fairway. 2. Lie about your handicap. 3. Instructions to the bartender at the 19th hole.

Set up. 1. How a player positions for an address. 2. A mistress who takes a cell phone picture of you naked while you catch a nap on her couch.

Shaft. 1. The part of the club joined to the head. 2. The part of the rod between the head and the balls. 3. What Tiger Woods may get if his wife doesn't take him back.

Shag. 1. To retrieve golf balls (American English). 2. Sexual intercourse (*British English*).

Shag hag. 1. Any container used by a golfer to hold practice balls (*American English*). 2. (*see* Shag, definition 2 (*British English*).

Shank. 1. A ball that caroms off the club and flies violently to the right. 2. (*see* Shag hag, definition 2 (British English). 3. A leg, bottom, or piece of meat.

Stop the bleeding. 1. To reverse a run of bad luck. 2. To seek medical aid after your wife shatters the rear windshield of your car upon discovering a girlfriend's name on your private caller ID.

Swing. 1. The graceful arc through which a club travels in completing any shot, including the take-away, backswing, topswing, downswing, point of impact, and follow through. 2. (*see* Shag, definition 2 (*British English*).

Tight. 1. A thin pad of grass between the ball and actual earth. 2. A player who makes very small or minuscule bets. 3. A player who relishes visits from the cart girl. 4. Players at the 19th hole at sunset. 5. When preceded with the preposition, "up," a wife who discovers a girlfriend's name on your caller ID. 6. A bad lie. 7. A good lay.

Top. 1. Hitting the ball above the center causing it to hop or roll rather than rise. 2. A bisexual preference not disclosed by a certain Tiger Woods mistress.

Trouble wood. 1. Any wood with a loft greater than that of a 5-wood. 2. *See* Woods, Tiger.

Up and down. 1. Getting up from a bunker and out of trouble in order to get down in the hole. 2. Hole action.

Waggle. 1. Rhythmic oscillation of the hips, legs, waist, arms, and club head to release tension and get the feel of the position. 2. Also used when addressing the ball in a golf game.

Ten Reasons Why Tiger Woods Confused Sex and Golf

1. A good lie gets you a good lay.

2. Threesomes and foursomes are easy to set up anywhere, anytime.

3. You can always choose the size of the shaft, which is particularly important in a threesome and you're said to be ambivalent.

4. You can muff a shot or take a shot at a muff.

5. You can clean your balls at every hole.

6. You always have your pick of public or private courses.

7. You can take just as many strokes as you want for any particular hole.

8. Tiger Woods likes his holes to be well trimmed.

9. The follow through makes all the difference and afterwards, you always feel you could have done a little bit better.

10. If you are Tiger Woods, good in bed and a pro in golf, you don't need any fucking lessons.

Ten Essential Excuses
for Playing Golf

1. If Tiger Woods isn't playing in the PGA, there are no golf tournaments on television worth seeing. Might as well go golfing myself.

2. I enjoy looking for my balls in the rough.

3. A golf course is nature's true church, and I can think of no greater religious experience than to do all of my praying on the fairway.

4. I enjoy hitting things.

5. I get great lawn care tips from the ground maintenance crews. There is nothing more inspiring than the smell of freshly cut grass.

6. I have been having trouble with my digestion lately. I think the exercise gained by walking 18 holes will help calm my stomach. Plus, I can pass gas without anyone knowing.

7. The beer cart girl is just graduating from community college, and I promised to give her some tips on finding a job.

8. My favorite caddy is just graduating from community college, and I promised to give him some tips on investing in stocks.

9. I'm between marriages.

10. I called in sick at work.

Tiger's Mistresses

Just how many mistresses are there? We know about the pancake house waitresses, the cocktails waitresses, the porn stars, the fitness buffs, the escorts, the New York night club butterfly: the list goes on. The tabloids are out there digging as much dirt as they can and between the ones who are known, those who want to be known and those who don't, no one really knows for sure how many mistresses he actually has.

Here is the tally at the beginning of 2010 and reported just as Tiger Woods was coming out of rehab.

1. Rachel Uchitel, 34, is a New York event planner and now a an entertainment show celeb. She has managed VIP action at clubs in New York, Las Vegas and the Hamptons. The reports are that when Elin left home, Tiger Woods would text Rachel, saying he wanted to be with her and send her messages such as "I love you, babe. It's always going to be just you and me."

2. Jaimee Grubbs is a Las Vegas reality show contestant and waitress to whom Woods sent a text message saying he would "wear you out." She sold her story of a 31-month-long affair to a tabloid.

3. Kalika Moquin is a third woman linked to Tiger Woods. A Las Vegas nightclub-marketing manager, she met with Woods several times at his hotel room one October weekend. He is reported to have told her that he was unhappy in his marriage and that he was under a lot of pressure.

4. Tiger Woods' alleged fourth mistress, Jamie Jungers, claims she had sex with Woods the night his father died. She is a Las Vegas lingerie model and waitress who claims an 18-month affair with Tiger Woods.

5. Mindy Lawton is a waitress in Orlando who told a tabloid that she had sex with Tiger Woods both at his mansion and in a church parking lot. Madly in love with Tiger, she said their affair ended just a few weeks before Woods' first child, a daughter, Sam, was born.

6. Cori Rist is a New York blonde and former dancer at the Penthouse Executive Club who secretly accompanied Tiger Woods on his tournaments and booked in the adjoining room to Tiger's so that the secrecy of their affair could be maintained. Although accused of being a $1,000-an-hour call girl, Cori told **New York Daily News** she was no prostitute and was never paid for any time she spent with Woods.

7. Holly Sampson, a porn star and a high profile escort, was the seventh alleged mistress who came forward. She probably can be safely said to have a strictly professional relationship with the golfer.

8. Unidentified female who is now in corporate position and wishes to keep her sexual relationship with the golfer confidential. There were indications that she may have hired attorney Michael O'Quinn to represent her.

9. An unidentified British television host who is said to be married now, although at the time of the affair with the master golfer she was single and ready to shag and drag.

10. Another unidentified female. If Tiger Woods is a sex-addicted cheetah, this woman may be his sex-addicted cougar.

11. Joslyn James is a thirty-two-year-old porn star. She also can claim to have a strictly professional relationship with the ace golfer.

12. Loredana Jolie [Ferriolo] is a Playboy model and escort. Hollywood Madam Michelle Braun, in an interview with the **New York Daily News**, said Loredana Jolie took part in group sex with Tiger Woods and paid as much as $15,000 for her participation. (*See* 18, on the next page.)

13. Theresa Rogers, a 48-year-old Florida blonde in incredible shape may hold the record for longevity of an alleged affair with Tiger Woods, traveling and sharing a bed with him for more than five years in a relationship that began before his marriage to Elin and continued after that, too. Gloria Allred, the attorney who represents Rachel Uchitel, is also her lawyer.

14. Julie Postle may be the "unidentified Orlando cocktail waitress," another of the Tiger's alleged mistresses. *The Hollywood Gossip* reported that Tiger told Postel that "his marriage was just for publicity . . . for image, entirely for the media and wasn't real."

15. Another unidentified female, who is also supposedly a lawyer and who wants to remain anonymous.

16. Jessica Simpson is a Hollywood actress. *Star Magazine* named Ms. Simpson in a "shocking story" it published alleging that she and Tiger Woods may have hooked up. Ms. Simpson denied the story and threatened a law suit. It may be entirely coincidental that both attended a golf tournament in Bethesda where they were photographed together.

17. Priyanka Chopra, Miss World and Bollywood actress. Did Tiger date Priyanka back in 2001 as reported before Elin Nordegren even met her future husband?

The controversy back then was that after India had two beauty pageant winners in Lara Dutton, Miss Universe, and Ms. Chopra, Miss World, Tiger may have had his eye on Lara, who was dating the New York Yankees Derek Jeter, a charge Tiger denied. But there were reports that in fact, the beauty queen that Tiger was dating was actually Ms. Chopra.

18. Men? Playboy model Loredana Jolie, who may be Mistress No. 12, or 11, or 10, made a claim in a *New York Post* page 6 story that took the sports world by surprise: Tiger Woods may be bisexual. In addition to girl-on-girl sex and threesomes, Jolie claims that Tiger had "sexual encounters with men."

Tiger Woods Jokes

From late night comics to Twitter, Facebook and, of course, the blogs, it took little time for the Tiger Woods jokes to begin circulating. While the professionals clearly sought to break new divots, the amateurs also had a field day. In fact, it was a chance for everyone to try their hand at writing jokes that practically wrote themselves. Here are a few of the best, or worse:

A Cheetah is the new Tiger.

Have you heard about the new Tiger Woods line of golf balls imprinted with the faces of his mistresses? Yeah. You, too, can drive them crazy.

"Last Friday, Tiger Woods hit a tree and a bunch of ladies fell out." --Seth Meyers on Weekend Update, Saturday Night Live.

The police asked Tiger's wife how many times she hit him. "I can't remember," she said. "Put me down for a five."

Tiger Wood's father was black and his mother from Thailand. Combined family reunions are Black-Thai affairs. - with a nod to comic Scott Doyle.

Phil Mickelson was on the phone to Elin Nordegren. He wanted to know if she had tips for beating Tiger.

Mistresses, what mistresses? Oh, you mean the provisionals?

Just came from the pro shop where they have Ping's new line of clubs, a set of irons. Yeah, they call 'em Elins. Guaranteed to beat Tiger.

Nike has a new motto: Just do me.

"Tiger always gives 110 percent. That is why he gave 100 percent to his wife and still had 10 percent left over for his alleged mistress." --Attributed to Steven Colbert.

"What does Tiger Woods have in common with a baby seal?" They've both been clubbed by a Norwegian. (Although Elin is Swedish, poetic license is sometimes taken with jokes.)

What's the difference between Tiger Woods and Santa Claus? Santa stopped at three ho's. –This has got to be one of the most posted jokes and twittered comments about the Tiger.

Tiger Woods is so rich that he owns lots of really expensive cars. Now, he even has a hole in one. –This one ties a close second with the following joke for most often posted.

Speaking of cars, what's the difference between a car and a golf ball? Tiger can drive a golf ball 400 yards.

Tiger Woods crashed into a fire hydrant and tree. Should have had a caddy to help him decide between an iron or a wood.

What in the world were Tiger and Elin doing out a 2:30 in the morning? They went clubbing.

Thank goodness Tiger Woods wasn't seriously injured in the crash, even though the experience still left him below par.

How does that golfer's motto go? "Never up, never in?"

Now that Tiger Woods has gone through sex rehab, how long will take him to get out of the woods for good?

Have any of his alleged mistresses revealed how many strokes it takes Tiger to get out of the bush?

Don't know how long it will last but there's a web site called www.tigerwodsjokes.org. It features David Letterman's Top Ten Ways Tiger Woods Can Improve His Image and a mildly amusing "Tiger Woods Christmas Song Parody." Among a bunch of jokes from Conan O'Brien is this one:

"The latest rumor is that one of Tiger's mistresses is a British sports broadcaster. Apparently, Tiger's nickname for her was The British Open."

About the Author

Dan Speers is the founding editor of *CitizenPoet.com*, the world's premier site for political poetry, daily epigrams, pithy satire and running commentary on the state of the world.

Visit *CitizenPoet* to read the latest "Takes" on the characters in the news: www.CitizenPoet.com

The secret's out: What really happened in the last days of the Bush presidency?

Plastic Explosives in Your Underwear? It's news to Homeland Security and the NSA, but not to Dan Speers. Early in 2009, Dan actually described the exact method a saboteur would use to blow up a plane in his book, *Master Spies Die Laughing*.

Dan describes how a combination of liquid, inflammable ribbon and plastic explosives could be hidden in the terrorist's panties and used to create a explosion that would bring down a passenger jet. Talk about your crotch rockets.

Turns out, truth is not only stranger than fiction, it's better.

In Pennsylvania, teenage students discovered that the cameras in their laptops that were furnished by their school could be turned on remotely and used to spy on whatever the students were doing at home—whether homework or changing clothes.

But it wasn't exactly a secret. Dan published a complete description of how spy chips were being secreted inside laptops over a year ago. All of the details are in the book.

And, yes, there's more. A whole lot more. Don't even think about waiting for the movie. This is one book you have to read now. *Master Spies Die Laughing* is the funniest spy novel you'll ever read. Available both in print and Kindle versions.

www.masterspies.com

Made in the USA
Charleston, SC
08 August 2010